RE

6.99

Buddhism for Today

Chris Wright

OXFORD
UNIVERSITY PRESS

About the series

We live in a world where there are people of many different religions. In many of our towns and cities Buddhists, Christians and Jews live alongside Muslims, Hindus and Sikhs. If you travel abroad, you will soon experience whole countries that have been shaped by religion.

We all have different ways of looking at things. It could be said that we all see the world through our own "spectacles". These spectacles are made up of our beliefs, opinions, attitudes and values. What is important to you might not be important to me.

Religious people see the world through their spectacles, which affects the way they see and live in the world. We can't understand someone else's worldview unless we look through their spectacles. The Religion For Today series helps you to do this by giving you the skills and knowledge to understand people with beliefs different from your own.

In learning about another religion you will also be given the chance to think about your own life. So you will not only learn about the religions you study; you will also learn from the religions.

Chris Wright, Series Editor

Languages of Buddhism

Buddhists have been happy to translate their holy books into the languages of countries into which Buddhism has spread. The Theravada scriptures were originally written down in Pali, whilst the Mahayana schools use sutras written Sanskrit. In this book we will use the Pali spellings, although the Sanskrit spellings of major words will also be included in the glossary.

Abbreviations

CE = Common Era
BCE = Before the Common Era.

About this book

In the last thirty years people in the West have become more informed about Buddhism. Because of travel to places like Burma, Thailand, Tibet, and Japan, Buddhist teachings have become more available and people are starting to find out more about the religion. In addition, many Buddhist "viharas" (temples or monasteries) have started to spring up in England.

Many people in the West who are caught up in the world of work and money have started to look for a different way of looking at life. In Buddhism they have found a way of seeing things which is centred on the spiritual journey for contentment and inner happiness. This book starts by introducing you to the life of Siddattha Gotama, the Buddha, who left his rich upbringing in order to search for contentment and inner peace.

The book will then introduce you to his teachings which have affected major world cultures and changed millions of lives over the last 2500 years. The Buddha never claimed that his teachings were original – in fact he made it clear that he taught an ancient path. These teachings are rooted in a basic observation: instead of running smoothly life is filled with so much misery ("dukkha", a word better translated as "unsatisfactoriness"). If you look around you, so many people seem to live unhappy lives; they don't appear to be content. The Buddha was like a doctor who looked at the worlds' ills and asked, "why is there so much suffering?", "what is it's cause?", and "how do we put an end to so much suffering?".

You will be encouraged to reflect on the "big questions" about suffering, life and death as well as learn about Buddhism as a major world religion today.

CONTENTS

GOING FOR REFUGE

Is there a special place you go to where you feel safe? Maybe there are certain people you always feel secure with. In this unit you will learn what it means for Buddhists to seek refuge and security in the Buddha, the Dhamma and the Sangha.

Buddhism is centred around three precious jewels. They are the **Buddha** (the historical man Siddattha Gotama who became the Buddha, the Enlightened One), the **Dhamma** (the Buddha's teaching) and the **Sangha** (the community of Buddhists). They are called jewels because they are the most important things in Buddhism. They are also referred to as the **Three Refuges**. A refuge is a place of safety in difficult times. When a person becomes a Buddhist he or she repeats the following three phrases:

▶ I go to the Buddha for refuge (three times).
▶ I go to the Dhamma for refuge (three times).
▶ I go to the Sangha for refuge (three times).

A monk in Thailand recites the Three Refuges in front of a statue of the Buddha. A statue of the Buddha is called a Buddha 'rupa'.

The Three Refuges can be repeated daily. Whenever Buddhists have ceremonies they will repeat them. The Buddhist Scriptures explain the importance of taking refuge:

> ❝ Men in their fear fly for refuge to mountains or forests, groves, sacred trees or shrines. But those are not a safe refuge, they are not the refuge that frees a man from sorrow. He who goes for refuge to Buddha, to Truth (Dhamma) and to those whom he taught (Sangha), he goes indeed to a great refuge. ❞
>
> [Dhammapada 188–90]

"Buddha" means "awakened" or "enlightened" one. It is a title not a name. It usually refers to the person who founded Buddhism – Siddattha Gotama. It also refers to the quality of inner awareness which we are all capable of having. When Buddhists say "I take refuge in the Buddha", they are expressing trust in their own capacity of being awake, of understanding.

The Buddha pointed out that seeing and following his teaching (Dhamma) was seeing and following him. The Dhamma is summed up in the Buddhist Scriptures in the following words: "Not to do any evil, to cultivate good, to purify one's mind, this is the teaching of the Buddha."

The importance of Buddhism

When a group of Buddhists were asked why it is important for people to find our about their religion they gave a number of reasons:

66 Whole countries have been affected by Buddhism. In some countries like Thailand and Burma it is the major religion. If we are to understand about these countries we need to understand about Buddhism. 99
[Jessica]

66 Buddhism is now well established in England as a major world religion. There are over 200 monasteries in Britain today. 99
[Juliet]

66 Buddhism challenges me to examine myself – my thoughts, feelings and emotions. Instead of just getting caught up in ugly emotions like jealousy, I am encouraged to examine the emotion and ask – what's causing this? 99
[Jane]

66 Buddhism offers people the opportunity to develop their minds through meditation. Meditation helps people to see things the way they really are. It helps develop concentration, awareness and self-awareness. I find meditation essential since I lead a very busy life. It is important to keep priorities right. 99
[Ian]

66 I especially like the Buddha's teachings on how to live. It is practical teaching about the problems which people face when trying to live their own lives. The Buddha never set down loads of rules but said "try it out, if it works follow it" and it works. 99
[Sylvia]

66 Buddhism has had a civilising effect on many people and countries. It teaches values of non-violence to all living things, including animals. 99
[Andrew]

1 Different people choose to seek refuge in different things.
(a) Why do you think some people think the following things give them refuge: money, a big house, a job with a large wage, a large family?
(b) Which, if any, of the above things do you think are a good refuge? Explain your answer.
(c) In what ways can people be refuges? Do you feel safe with a particular person? Why?

2 As a class, collect on the board all the things you already know about Buddhism. Have any of you met a Buddhist monk or nun? What did you think?

3 Write a sentence on each of the following: Three Refuges, Buddha, Dhamma, Sangha.

4 Look at the reasons given for studying Buddhism. Put them in order with what you consider to be the most important reason at the top of the list and the least important at the bottom. Compare your list with a partner and explain your choice.

SIDDATTHA GOTAMA

The life story of the historical Buddha is of a prince who became a poor man in order to discover the source of true happiness. In this unit we shall be discussing whether money and fame can bring happiness.

The man who became known as the Buddha was called Siddattha Gotama. It is generally held that he was born about 563 BCE in a village called Lumbini near the modern border between India and Nepal. His father ruled a tribe called the Shakyas. Siddattha was brought up as a Hindu prince in the greatest luxury and splendour.

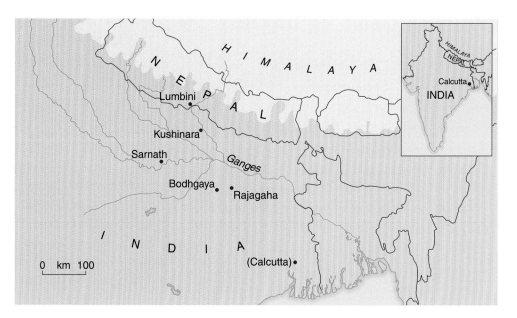

A map of the north-east India and Nepal, showing important sites in the life of the Buddha.

A wise man had prophesied to his parents that when Siddattha grew up he would become either a great ruler, like his father, or else a homeless holy man. His father didn't want Siddattha to become a homeless wanderer. He tried to do everything in his power to stop Siddattha asking questions that would encourage him to go in search of the meaning of life. Siddattha was protected against seeing anything that was ugly in life. He was brought up in a palace surrounded by beautiful things, a place in which suffering was kept hidden. He was totally unaware of how different life was for most people beyond the walls of the palace. A story is even told of how his father employed numerous gardeners so that Siddattha would not even see anything dying in the natural world.

When he was 16 Siddattha married. He also had a harem of beautiful dancers. As he himself admits, "I was spoiled, very spoiled." Yet he called his only son "Rahula", which means chains, for in the middle of all this luxury he felt as if he were in chains; he was restless — life gave him no satisfaction.

1 *Where did Siddattha come from? Which religion did he belong to? Why did his father try to protect him from seeing any form of suffering in the world? Was Siddattha happy with the life he lived in the palace?*

2 (a) Which of the following things do you think are important for happiness: money, fame, good looks, IQ of 160, true friends, sex appeal, something else (add your own)?

(b) Which is most important to you? Give a reason why.

Siddattha was like some of the rich and famous people who are alive today. Although they have wealth they are still not happy. Life does not satisfy them. As a class brainstorm the names of famous people who in one sense "have everything" but are still not happy. How do you know they are not happy?

▶ This is a Buddha rupa in Burma. Why do you think Siddattha is shown with beautiful hair and long ear lobes? How do these show his princely upbringing?

MY DRINK AND DRUGS HELL

"I am Tom and I am an addict"

Leading drummer Tom Thumper talks for the first time about his drinks and drugs nightmare that nearly destroyed him and finally forced him to seek a cure in America. Britain's best-loved drummer admits: "In my free time off stage I drank, took Valium, painkillers, marijuana, and finally I couldn't control it. I suppose it began on my holidays – I can't handle holidays so I used to drink to fill up my time." Thumper explained he felt unloved by his mother as a child, claiming she thought of him as a "misfit". He thumped drums instead of hitting back at school bullies.

Thumper has spent the last three weeks in a drug clinic in America drying out. Patients are there because alcohol and drugs have made their lives miserable and unmanageable. Last week he admitted: "I have learned a lot. I have learned how to have a different attitude to life, which is wonderful. I have got fed up with running."

3 (a) Why do you think Tom Thumper was not happy?

(b) How do you think he would describe happiness? Is this definition different from yours – if so, in what way?

(c) What do you think he means when he says? "I have learned how to have a different attitude to life ... I have got fed up with running"?

4 Why do you think Siddattha called his son Rahula?

THE FOUR SIGHTS OF SUFFERING

When Siddattha was 29 years old he became aware of all the suffering in the world. In this unit you will be looking at how people suffer and the questions that people ask when they are suffering.

Siddattha became curious to find out more about life as it was lived outside the palace walls. When he was 29 years old he decided to take a ride in his chariot through the city near where he lived. As they journeyed along they saw four sights.

Sight 1

Prince: *(pointing to an old man)* What is the matter with that man, charioteer?

Charioteer: He is old, my lord. That is all.

Prince: All?

Charioteer: Old age does that to everyone.

Prince: Does old age always destroy beauty, youth and strength?

Charioteer: Yes, my lord.

Prince: Drive back to the palace at once. How can I enjoy the journey when my heart is afraid of old age?

▶ *What do you feel when you look at these pictures of Winston Churchill? How did he change as he grew older? What might anyone feel about becoming old, losing health, strength and good looks?*

Sight 2

Narrator: The next day, the Prince made another journey. Once again, the prince's attention was attracted by a person at the roadside.

Prince *(pointing to a leper):* What is the matter with that man?

Charioteer: That, my lord, is a leper. That is what sickness can do to a man.

▶ *This picture shows lepers in Mali. Have you ever been really ill? What does it feel like? Which illness frightens you most?*

Sight 3

Narrator: On his third journey, the Prince hoped to see no more suffering.

Prince: What is that? What do those men carry?

Charioteer: That, my lord, is a dead man.

Prince: Do we all end up like that?

Charioteer: Yes, my lord, we shall all die.

▶ *What is happening in this picture? What feelings do you have as you study the picture? Why do you have these feelings?*

Sight 4

Narrator: The Prince decided to make just one more journey outside the palace grounds. On this occasion he saw a wandering holy man. He was alone and dressed in rags, and clearly owned nothing.

Prince: What is that man?

Charioteer: He is a holy man.

Prince: Although he has nothing and is old and poor he is happy. Why is this?

Charioteer *(pointing to the holy man):* Perhaps he has discovered some secret; perhaps old age, sickness and death are no longer frightening for him.

Narrator: Siddattha was distressed. He had become aware of all the suffering which exists in the world. He had also been shown a solution to it – the holy man had shown him how to be contented and happy in such a suffering world.

Prince: I must leave this palace of illusions and go in search of the way to end all this suffering.

Narrator: Around midnight he slipped away from the palace to go in search of the happiness he saw in the holy man.

1 *What forms of suffering did Siddattha experience when he journeyed outside the palace? What thoughts might have gone through his mind when he saw these sights?*

2 *What Siddattha experienced happens to us all. Sometime in our lives we wake up to the fact that we too are going to suffer. Today people only have to turn on the television to see suffering in all its ugly forms being acted out on the news every single day. In groups make a collage to illustrate Siddattha's discovery that life is full of suffering.*

This old man is sweeping the grounds outside a temple as an act of dedication. He is poor – but perhaps he is contented.

Siddattha Searches for Happiness

Siddattha's charioteer drove him into the forest. There Siddattha took off his royal clothes and cut off his rich black hair with a sword as a sign that he had given up all worldly pleasures and riches.

At first he decided to try a traditional Hindu way to truth. He had discovered that riches did not make him happy so he tried an opposite way. He denied himself all luxuries and attempted to live on little food. He practised strict religious disciplines, trying to control his body in order to control pain and suffering. He practised so hard that at one stage he was eating only one grain of rice each day. He came to look just like a skeleton. One day he collapsed. This led him to conclude that this was not the way to happiness. Clearly one's body could not escape disease, old age and death.

Siddattha became so thin that by pressing his stomach he could feel his spine. He and the other ascetics were trying to conquer suffering by making their minds so strong that they would forget about their bodies.

1 *Imagine that you are Siddattha, living in the modern world, on the night he leaves home in search of happiness. What would you say to your wife on the phone if you rang her to explain what you are doing and why? In pairs rehearse the conversation and then write it down.*

The Middle Way

He had now lived in the luxury of a palace and at the edge of starvation but his unhappiness was as great as ever. One day in the forest he was approached by a lady who, seeing him near starvation, offered him some rice. He began to eat a little and try a "Middle Way" between the extremes of having everything and having nothing. The five holy men he had been training with were disappointed at his "softness" and left him.

He went and sat at the foot of a tree and made a promise to himself that he would not move until he had found the answers to the questions he was asking:

▶ "Why is there suffering?"
▶ "Where is true happiness to be found?"

The ancient stories say that as he sat and meditated he was tempted to give up his efforts by Mara. (Mara is the force of darkness – all that disturbs and poisons our minds: greed, anger and confusion.)

Firstly he was tempted by desire in the form of beautiful women to give up his search and return to the luxurious life of the palace. Then he was tempted by fear to give up. However, Siddattha was determined not to be distracted. "Let my skin wither, my hands grow numb, my bones dissolve. Until I have gained understanding I will not rise from here."

Silently he lifted his right hand from his lap, reached in front of him and touched the earth. The earth itself was his witness that he would sit through all distractions until he found peace and happiness.

2 (a) *In pairs discuss what it feels like to be tested or tempted, e.g. by fear when you are alone in the house at night, or by distractions to give up when you are trying to work or revise for an exam. What are you tempted by? What stops you from concentrating?*

(b) *In pairs sit back to back. One person imagines they are the temptation itself. The other person is the target of the temptation. By passing a piece of paper back to each other have a conversation. Once you have written it act it out in front of the class.*

The Buddha being tempted by Mara.

FIVE

THE ENLIGHTENMENT

As Siddattha meditated he had an amazing experience. In this unit you will find out about this experience, called the Enlightenment. You will also look at experiences we have which make us see things in a different way. You will ask the question "what can I learn from these experiences?"

Look carefully at this picture. What do you see? Share your descriptions with the class.
- *Did you see a young woman or an old hag?*
- *Now can you see both?*
Pictures like these are called optical illusions and can be seen in a number of ways.

Siddattha's Enlightenment

When people suddenly see something in a different way they experience what has been called an "aha" feeling. They see what is really there. Some people experience this when a friend does something they didn't expect (e.g. being really nice to someone who is being bullied). From that moment on their opinion of their friend changes and they treat them differently. People suddenly see what has been in front of them all of the time. It is like a mist clearing.

Siddattha experienced a similar illumination as he meditated under the Bodhi tree. For the first time he saw the world as it really was. This event is called his "Enlightenment" – a word which draws attention to the fact that he saw the light. It is said that Siddattha became awakened – he woke up to the nature of the world: what causes suffering and how to bring an end to suffering. From now on he became known as "the Buddha" (the Enlightened One). At the heart of his Enlightenment was the discovery that everything is linked in a chain of cause and effect.

The Buddha is often shown sitting on a lotus blossom. For Buddhists the lotus is a symbol of Enlightenment. The roots of the lotus grow in muddy water just as our minds are darkened by things like anger and greed. The flower rises up out of the water and gradually opens its petals as it faces the sun. So also the mind can become enlightened.

1. *Look back at the case of Tom Thumper (page 7). What links can you make in his life story? For example, why did he become a drummer? What caused him to drink so much?*

2. *Draw the lotus flower and roots.*
   (a) The lotus grows out of mud. What things in life drag you down? List:
      ▶ *the feelings you have*
      ▶ *the things which happen to you.*
      Label these on the bottom part of your drawing.
   (b) The lotus flower blossoms in the sun. What things in life draw the best out of you? List:
      ▶ *the things people could say to you*
      ▶ *the things which happen to you.*
      Label these on the top part of your drawing.

3. *You have been asked by a local television station to produce a 45-second commercial explaining what Siddattha experienced in his Enlightenment. How would you get across the idea of Enlightenment? What pictures would you use to show how people can suddenly start to look at things in a different way?*

SIX

THE BUDDHA TEACHES

After becoming enlightened the Buddha taught others what he had discovered. In this unit you will be asking what makes a good teacher and looking at the practical way in which the Buddha taught.

"Having myself crossed the ocean of suffering I must help others to cross it. Freed myself, I must set others free." The Buddha became enlightened when he was 35 years old. For the next forty-five years he travelled around northern India teaching others the truth about the way things are in the world. His teaching is called the Dhamma.

He was not concerned about providing answers to questions such as "when did the universe begin?" He felt these questions did not help people to stop suffering. He told the parable of the arrow to illustrate the practical nature of his teaching.

1 ▶ *In groups make a list of ten qualities of a good teacher.*
When the Buddha taught he:
- *explained things clearly*
- *related what he said to everyday life*
- *was a very practical teacher. He wanted people to learn and find out things for themselves.*
- *adapted what he said to the interests and abilities of the different people he talked to.*

2 ▶ *Look at the parable of the arrow.*
(a) Why, why, why? Make a list of "why questions" that people ask. Are they helpful questions? Divide them into which are possible and useful to answer and which are not.
(b) Are you satisfied with what the Buddha said was more important? Explain your answer.

The parable of the arrow

❝ Suppose a man is wounded by a poisoned arrow, and his friends and relatives bring him to a surgeon. Suppose the man should then say: "I will not let this arrow be taken out until I know who shot me; I will not let this arrow be taken out until I know the kind of bow with which I was shot … the kind of bowstring used and the type of arrow … what sort of feather was used on the arrow and with what kind of material the point of the arrow was made." That man would die without knowing any of these things.

Even so, if anyone says, "I will not follow the holy life until I have answers to questions such as whether the universe is eternal or not, or what happens after I die, or is there a God", he would die with these questions unanswered. What is truly important is to know the nature of suffering and the way to overcome it. ❞
[Samyutta Nikaya]

This Indian Buddha rupa from about the third century BCE is in the British Museum. It shows the Buddha teaching. His hands are in the gesture known as Dhammacakra.

"Come and see for yourself"

The Buddha said that his teaching was to be tried out in life. It was a practical way to overcome suffering and to find true happiness. He taught people not to believe what he told them just because he said it, but to test his teaching in their own experience and follow it if it proved true. "It is often said that the Buddha's teaching is only a raft to help you cross the river, a finger pointing to the moon. Don't mistake the finger for the moon. The raft is not the shore." It has also been said of the Buddha's teaching: "A knowledge of the path cannot be substituted for putting one foot in front of the other!" Read this story about an explorer:

The explorer

A story is told of how one day an explorer returned to his people who were eager to know about the Amazon. But how could he put into words all the wonderful things he had seen: the feelings that flooded his heart when he saw exotic flowers and heard the nightsounds of the forests; when he sensed the danger of wild beasts or paddled his canoe over treacherous rapids?

He said, "Go and find out for yourselves". To guide them he drew a map of the river. They pounced upon the map. They framed it in their Town Hall. They made copies of it for themselves. And all who had a copy considered themselves experts on the river, but did they know its every turn and bend, how broad it was, how deep, where the rapids were and where the falls?

3 Look at the story of the explorer.
   (a) If you met the explorer what would you want to know?
   (b) What would you like to say to the people he gave the map to?
   (c) Why do you think the people framed the map?
   (d) This is not just a story about the Amazon. It tells you things about people's attitude to life. What do you think the map stands for? Who do the people stand for?

THE BUDDHA DIES

The Buddha died of food poisoning when he was 80 years old. Ananda, his chief disciple, cried: "O Buddha please do not leave us! For so many years you have been our guide. What shall we do without you?" The Buddha answered, "Dear Ananda, I have always taught that death is a natural part of life. It is nothing to fear. When I am gone, let my teachings be your guide. If you have understood them in your heart, you have no more need of me."

Although the Buddha died, his Dhamma (teaching) and the Sangha (community of his followers) had successfully taken root.

The Buddha always stressed that he was not a god to be worshipped. Instead he focused people's attention upon his teaching:

Monk: Are you a god?
Siddattha: No.
Monk: Are you a saint?
Siddattha: No.
Monk: Then what are you?
Siddattha: I am awake.

The Buddha died at Kushinara, in northern India. Today it is an important place of pilgrimage for Buddhists. Because he died lying on his side between two trees many statues show him in that position.

The Buddha's body was cremated and the remains were divided. They were sent to various places, including Lumbini, Bodhgaya, Sarnath and Kushinara, the four key pilgrimage sites. A burial mound called a stupa was built over each portion of the remains. Today Buddhists go on special journeys, called pilgrimages, to places connected with the Buddha's life. At these places they will see stupas and also images of the Buddha.

1 *What happened to the Buddha at the four key pilgrimage places? Draw the map of India and Nepal on page 6. Using this unit and the index to help you, write short notes on each place on your map.*

2 *If possible, talk to a Buddhist about what it felt like to go on pilgrimage. Why did they go? What are the benefits?*

3 *Imagine that you are a Buddhist going on pilgrimage to one of the four key sites. Using other books to help you, draw and write a postcard back home. You may want to:*
- *describe what you see*
- *express what you feel*
- *say why it is important for you to visit this place.*

4 *(a) What things do people bring back from their holidays? Why do they do this?*
(b) Buddhists also bring back things when they return from a pilgrimage. Why do you think they do this? What things do you think they bring back which cannot be bought with money?

The Buddha's eyes were opened about the way things were in the world under a Bodhi tree at Bodhgaya. Today Bodhgaya in north-east India is a place of pilgrimage.

THREE MARKS OF LIFE

In units 8, 9 and 10 you will be considering the Three Marks of Life.

The Buddha became enlightened to the way things are in the world. He called his discovery the Three Marks of Life. They are:

1 **Anicca** – everything changes and nothing lasts for ever
2 **Dukkha** – life is unsatisfactory
3 **Anatta** – there is no such thing as the self

Carefully consider each of the Three Marks of Life over the next six pages. As you study them, ask yourself whether they are true.

First Mark of Life: Anicca
Everything changes and nothing lasts for ever.

1 In groups:
(a) Make a list of things which do change, e.g. fashions in clothes, pop music, seasons, people.
(b) Try to name something in the world which does not change. Is there anything?

Impermanence

Remember this now
To save all the trouble,
Life is a rainbow,
Life is a bubble.

Everything changes
Nothing's the same,
First there is sunshine
And then there is rain.

First there are smiles
Then there are tears,
Things last for a while
And then disappear.

Sad becomes happy,
Rain becomes fine.
Minutes are hours,
So goes the time.

Life is not good,
But life is not bad
Everything happens
Both happy and sad.

Everything changes
So everyone's free
Don't cling to wishes,
Just live now and be.

2 Carefully read the poem "Impermanence".
(a) Use a dictionary to find out what this word means.
(b) Illustrate the verses of the poem with words and pictures or photographs. For example, for the third verse you could write about a situation in which happiness turns into sadness, such as friends falling out.

In the natural world Anicca can be illustrated by frogspawn turning into tadpoles which then turn into frogs.

3 ▶ (a) Collect pictures from magazines to make a collage to illustrate the first Mark of Life.
OR
(b) Design a logo for a badge of life to show that everything changes, e.g. a seed developing into a plant which then produces flowers; new cars ending up on scrap heaps and their metal being recycled.

COMING TO TERMS WITH SUFFERING

Why do you think that people have to suffer? The Buddha taught that suffering was part of the way things were in life. In this unit you will be considering what he meant when he taught that life itself was unsatisfactory.

Second Mark of Life: Dukkha

Life is unsatisfactory.

The Buddha is often compared to a doctor who diagnoses the suffering of the world and then offers a cure. His diagnosis is summed up in the Four Noble Truths.

1 *When people are ill they often go to a doctor to find out why they are suffering. Write down what the doctor does when he or she sees the patient. Try to include all the steps from identifying the illness to prescribing the cure.*

The Four Noble Truths

1 **Dukkha is part of everyday life:**
First the Buddha observed what was happening in the world. Instead of running smoothly, life is filled with the miseries of birth, old age, sickness and death. If I am happy with a friend, then when that friend goes I am sad. If I crave something badly, that is a form of suffering. Even when I have everything I am afraid that I might lose it – I am not happy. We will never be happy if our happiness is based on things which change. This suffering is called Dukkha, a word which suggests restlessness and unsatisfactoriness. This is the *First Noble Truth* (see opposite).

2 *With a friend make a list of five things which make you happy. Take it in turns to argue as a Buddhist that these things only offer temporary happiness but don't actually fully satisfy you.*

2 **The cause of suffering:**
Then the Buddha diagnosed the cause of Dukkha. We experience Dukkha because we are always craving. Some people show this attitude in relation to their jobs: they become completely ambitious, always wanting to do better, never content. This is the *Second Noble Truth* (see page 24).

3 **How to end Dukkha:**
If the cause of Dukkha is craving, the end of Dukkha is obvious – stop craving. This is the *Third Noble Truth* (see page 26).

4 **The cure of suffering:**
The Buddha gave people the prescription for their cure. This is the Fourth Noble Truth. The Buddha taught that people can practise letting go of craving by following certain moral and spiritual disciplines. He summed these up in the *Noble Eightfold Path* (see page 28).

The First Noble Truth

The Buddha taught in many ways: through the example of his own life, through telling stories and through solving people's problems. In the following account the Buddha taught a woman, Gotami, by giving her a task to perform.

The story of Kisa Gotami and the mustard seed

On one occasion a woman called Gotami came to the Buddha in tears, holding the body of her dead baby son. She was so upset that she had gone everywhere to try to bring him back to life. Her friends felt sorry for her and told her to go to see the Buddha. She came before the Buddha still holding the child in her arms. "Please bring him back to life for me," she cried. Very gently the Buddha answered: "I can help you, Gotami, but first you must bring me something. I need one small mustard seed. However, it must come from a house where no one has ever died."

Gotami quickly went in search of a mustard seed. She asked at one home and the woman there answered, "Of course you can have a mustard seed. You can have whatever you want, but you should know that last year my husband died." "Oh," Gotami replied, "then I must continue my search elsewhere," and ran off to the next house. But wherever she went the same thing happened. Everyone wanted to help her but in every family she visited someone had died. One person told her, "Three years ago my daughter died." Another said, "My brother died here yesterday." It was always the same.

At the end of the day she returned to the Buddha. "What have you found Gotami?" he asked. "Where is your mustard seed? And where is your son? You are not carrying him any longer." She answered, "Oh Buddha, today I have discovered that I am not the only one who has lost a loved one. Everywhere people have died. I see how foolish I was to think I could have my son back. I have accepted his death and this afternoon I cremated him. Now I have returned to you to hear your teachings. I am ready to listen."

The Buddha said, "Gotami, you have learned a great deal today. Suffering and death must come to everyone sooner or later. But if you can learn the truth you can live and die in happiness. Come I shall teach you." And so he taught her, and soon she found more peace than she had ever known before.

3 (a) How did you feel when you read this story? Do you think that the Buddha acted in a kind way?

(b) Which of the Buddha's Noble Truths had Gotami learnt in this practical lesson?

(c) When Gotami first went to the Buddha he replied: "I can help you, Gotami."
- What sort of help did Gotami expect?
- What sort of help did she receive? Explain carefully how they differ.
- How did the Buddha's way of teaching illustrate what was said on pages 14–15?

(d) What was the cause of her suffering? How did she stop her own suffering?

(e) Act this story out.

TEN
WHAT AM I?

Just as everything in nature changes so also people change continually. This is known as the third Mark of Life.

Third Mark of Life: Anatta

There is no such thing as the self.

1
(a) *Think about ways in which you are changing (e.g. emotions, body). Is there any part of you which is not changing?*

(b) *Write the story of the life of a person as if it were to take place in one day. For example, they would reach middle age at about lunch-time. Listen to some of the stories in class. What can you say about the nature of life from these stories?*

2
If everything is changing who is the real you? How would you describe yourself? Draw the shape of a human being and label it to say who you are.

If you stop and think about how we talk about ourselves, you will notice that we speak as if there is an inner part of us which owns all of the parts. For example, we say "My fears", "My headache", "My future". Who is this "My" we keep talking about? Does it really exist?

▶ *These pictures show the same person as a baby, a teenager, and a middle-aged woman. Do you think there is any part of this person which stays the same? Compare a photograph of yourself as a baby and one as you are now. How have you changed? Are you the same person? Which is the real "me"?*

3 Write a diary for today describing the different emotions/feelings you have. Say what made your feel like this.

4 In ten years time will you be the same person as you are now? What will have changed? Why will you have changed?

5 Imagine a time in the future when it is possible to do brain transplants of people in serious accidents. If a person has a brain transplant will they still be the same person? What about a heart transplant?

The chariot and its parts

One of the Buddha's followers, Nagasena, compared who we are with a chariot. A chariot is made up of many different parts, said Nagasena. If you take the chariot to pieces you can call these parts by their different names: axle, wheel, shaft, carriage. But there is no "thing" among these parts called a chariot. A chariot is only the name we give it when all of these parts are brought together. The chariot disappears when it is taken to pieces. It is not a "thing" in its own right at all.

Now think about the thing you call "myself". Like the chariot it is made up of many parts. But what happens when you take the parts to pieces? What are you left with? What you have are: body, feelings, thoughts, instincts and understanding.

There is, however, said Nagasena, no actual thing called a self. He went on to say that when death separates these parts there is nothing left. What you call "myself" is not a "thing" at all. It does not exist.

This Persian model of a chariot dates from about the fifth century BCE.

6 Discuss what you think of Nagasena's comparison of the human person with a chariot.

23

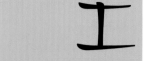 WANT, I WANT, I WANT

In this unit you will be exploring what the Buddha taught in the Second Noble Truth, about the cause of suffering. (Look back to page 20 to remind yourself about the Four Noble Truths.)

1 What things were being advertised on television last night?
(a) In groups try to make a list of fifteen things.
(b) Which was the best commercial? Why?
(c) What idea of "happiness" were these commercials trying to get across?

Everyday commercials and advertisements on television and in magazines encourage people to want new things. It encourages an "I want, want, want" mentality. The Buddha gave this feeling a name. He called it **tanha**. It is a thirst or craving for things.

2 (a) What do you feel when you don't get what you want? How long do these feelings last?
(b) What do you feel when somebody breaks or loses something which belongs to you?

People don't just want objects. They also get attached to certain feelings. This is also tanha. The different ways in which people crave (tanha) can be illustrated by a story called 'The wagons of life'. Read it on the page opposite, then answer the questions below.

3 The Old Woman described the four wheels as standing for four things people need in life.
(a) Copy down these four things and give examples of each:
Bodily needs: e.g. clothes ...
Love: e.g. of parents ...
Worldly aims: e.g. to get on with friends ...
Spiritual aims: e.g. to be good ...
(b) Which of these do you think is the most important and the least important? Say why.

4 The Old Woman said that people pile up their wagons so much that they break.
(a) Make a list of things which people "pile up their wagons with".
(b) Give an example of what she might mean when she says that their wagons sometimes break.

5 The Old Man explains why people pile up their wagons when he says "It is part of their mentality".
(a) What word would the Buddhist use to describe this craving?
(b) Do you agree with the Old Man's description of people's attitude to life? Give reasons and examples to back up what you say.

The wagons of life

Narrator: One night two children came to a beautiful little farmhouse, completely surrounded by piles of wagon wheels. An old couple opened the door and invited them in. They went to look at the wheels more closely and then saw that behind the farmhouse was a collection of wagons.

Child 1: Have you made them?

Old Man: Yes we have.

Child 2: But why? For whom?

Old Man: For those who journey on the path of life.

Old Woman: Each of these wagons has four wheels. The first is the wheel of bodily needs: that is, being free from hunger, illness and cold. The second is the wheel of love, made of two halves put together – loving and being loved. The third is the wheel of worldly aims. These are the goals which give a sense of direction to life. They change as you grow through different stages of life. The fourth wheel is the wheel of spiritual aims, those beyond the limited reality of this world. It is towards that goal that people should really be moving. Sadly people pile up their wagons with so many things they think they need that they end up breaking their wagons and they have to come back to have them repaired.

Child 2: Can you repair the wheels for them?

Old Man: (sadly) Not always. The wheels of health and love are often very difficult to make strong again.

Child 1: But why do people want to carry so much?

Old Man: Because they believe they need everything they see or hear about. But there are worse things than that. It is part of their mentality that each year they must want certain things and obtain them, and that the next year they must have even more.

Child 1: How mad! But what can we do to help the adults?

Old Woman: You must show them that all they pile up on their wagons, although it is very pleasant, is not really what they need in life. They are only the playthings of life.

Child 2: Do adults really attach so much importance to these things?

Old Woman: They are ready to die for them, and in taking them with them on life's journey they do die. If what you want is heavier than what you have, you are in a low position and unsatisfied. But if what you want is less than what you have, you will be in a high position and very satisfied.

SIMPLY LET GO

In this unit you will explore the Third Noble Truth and ask whether by stopping craving you also stop Dukkha. (Look back to page 20 to remind yourself about the Four Noble Truths.)

1 *What makes people want things? In groups make up a list of reasons.*

The Buddha identified three reasons why people want things:

1 **Greed** – A desire for pleasure.
2 **Hatred** – Not liking things and wanting to get rid of them.
3 **Ignorance** – By not understanding myself properly I misunderstand the world. I grasp at what is impermanent, thinking it will bring me lasting happiness. One Buddhist teacher talked about it in this way:

66 The desire for happiness kicks from one side; dissatisfaction and fear kick from the other. Don't you see? If you follow these extremes, you will simply strike out when you are angry and grab for what attracts you. How long can you go on being trapped in this way? 99
[Ajahn Chah, A Still Forest Pool]

2 (a) *Make a list of emotions. Pick out the three most powerful emotions and talk about them with a partner. Why are these emotions powerful? How do they illustrate what Ajahn Chah says?*

(b) *Prepare a 30-second television commercial to show the effects of greed, hatred and ignorance in the world today. What pictures would you show? What would be your commentary?*

Learning to let go

The Buddha said that greed and hatred could be our teachers because it is only when we understand how they work within us that we can learn how to deal with them, instead of being controlled by them. He went on to teach that there is a way out of wanting and suffering, and that is to simply let go. Read this story:

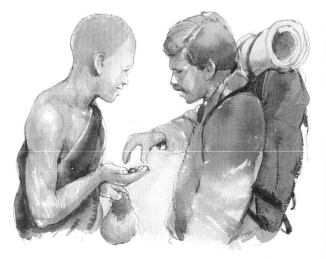

A monk in his travels once found a precious stone and kept it. One day he met a traveller, and when the monk opened his bag to share his food with him, the traveller saw the jewel and asked the monk to give it to him. The monk did so happily. The traveller went on his way overjoyed. The precious jewel would give him enough wealth and security for the rest of his life. However, a few days later he came back in search of the monk, found him and gave back the stone. He begged the monk, "Now give me something much more precious than this stone, valuable as it is. Give me that which made you able to give it to me."

In the story the traveller wanted to know the secret of how to let go of things, how to stop wanting things. One way of doing this is to practise acts of generosity and kindness towards people. In 1993 a book was published in America called Random Acts of Kindness. Within months it sold an amazing 200,000 copies. This is one of the stories of kindness in the book:

> 66 I have been going to the same coffee shop every Sunday for years. One morning in the middle of a great dreary drizzly weekend, I went in dripping wet and ordered my usual doughnut and coffee. I was casually told that my coffee had already been paid for. I looked around expecting to see some friend sitting somewhere but didn't. When I asked, the young woman at the cash desk just smiled and said someone paid for twenty coffees and you are number eight. I sat there for almost an hour, reading my paper, and watching more surprised people come in to find their morning coffee prepaid. There we all were with big funny smiles on our faces, looking at everyone else in the restaurant trying to figure out who had done this incredible thing, but mostly just enjoying the experience as a group. It was a beautiful blast of sunshine on an otherwise wet winter's day. 99

3 (a) If you were in the coffee shop what feelings might you have?

(b) What qualities would be required of the person who did this act of kindness?

(c) In groups think up your own acts of kindness and collect the ideas of the class on the board. Put together a booklet of things you could do, or have done, or have heard about.

4 Carry out one act of kindness today. Remember, to really let go you should not let on that you have done it. Write up a diary account of what you did and what effect it had on the other person.

5 Why do you think some people are afraid of letting go and being generous?

6 Name five ways in which the world would be different if more people let go of greed and hatred and practised acts of kindness and generosity. You could make up your own newspaper front page.

THE NOBLE EIGHTFOLD PATH

Over the next five units we will be exploring the Buddha's teaching on the Fourth Noble Truth: how to come to terms with suffering. It is called the Noble Eightfold Path.

The story of the raft

66 A man is on a journey. He comes to a vast stretch of water. On this side the shore is dangerous, but on the other it is safe. No boat goes to the other shore, nor is there any bridge. He thinks, "It would be good if I could make a raft, and with the help of the raft cross over safely to the other side, exerting myself with my hands and feet." Having crossed over and got to the other side, he thinks, "This raft was of great help to me. It would be good if I carry this raft on my head wherever I go."

What do you think – would that man be acting properly with regard to the raft? In the same manner, I have taught a doctrine similar to a raft – it is for crossing over, and not for carrying. 99

[Majjhima Nikaya]

1 ▶ Look at the picture.
(a) If the water stands for human life, what events in life might
  ▶ a rough sea be describing?
  ▶ a calm sea be describing?
(b) If the water is you
  ▶ what thoughts and feelings might a rough sea be describing?
  ▶ what thoughts and feelings might a calm sea be describing?

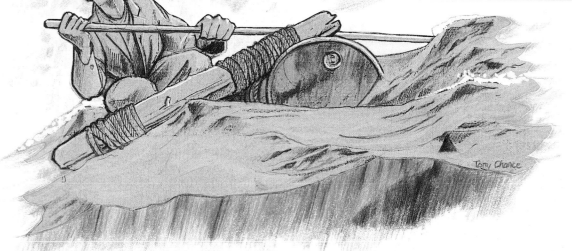

The Buddha compared his teaching to a raft on the sea of life. Sometimes life is stormy, at other times it is calm. He taught that people need a raft to take them out of the stormy waters of life. He described this raft in his Fourth Noble Truth in which he offered the way to end craving. The Fourth Noble Truth is called the Noble Eightfold Path.

3 Right Speech

Words are very powerful things. You should take care in what you say – make sure that all you say is helpful and encourages goodness.

2 Right Attitude

Your mental attitude to life affects what you get out of life. Developing right attitudes and thoughts is important.

4 Right Action

The Buddha taught, "Let a man overcome evil by good." You should behave in ways which are kind and compassionate.

5 Right Livelihood

You must be careful to have a job which does not destroy life or cause harm to others.

1 Right Understanding

Seeing the world as it is (unsatisfactory) and understanding that there is a path to freedom.

6 Right Effort

Making an effort to be mindful of what you do, say and think. Making an effort not to become attached to harmful thoughts and desires, and seeking good thoughts.

8 Right Concentration

Having understood that life is full of suffering, this step aims at letting go of all desires and cravings and so to stop suffering.

7 Right Awareness

You must be totally alert to life, aware of what you are doing, its possible results and the reason why you are doing it.

The Buddha taught that by treading this Noble Path a person might achieve a state of bliss, happiness and peace, free from Dukkha. This state of bliss is **Nibbana** (see page 39).

2 (a) Copy the diagram of the Noble Eightfold Path into your books.
(b) In pairs discuss how you would change if you tried to keep the Eightfold Path. Which of the steps would you find most difficult? Explain why.

3 (a) How would your school have to change if it was going to put the Noble Eightfold Path into practice?
(b) Make a list of rules for a school that is attempting to follow the Noble Eightfold Path.

4 Make a collage using newspapers to show how the Noble Eightfold Path has things to teach the world today. Try to choose a news story to illustrate the relevance of each of the eight steps.

RIGHT UNDERSTANDING, ATTITUDE AND SPEECH

In this unit we will be considering the first three elements of the Noble Eightfold Path.

Right Understanding

The first step towards Enlightenment is to have a correct understanding of the world – to realise that life is unsatisfactory (full of Dukkha). This is to understand the Four Noble Truths (look back to page 20).

Right Attitude

Your mental attitude to life affects what you get out of it. For example, if you go through life being miserable and angry you will only get misery and anger back in return. But if you develop love and kindness you will be rewarded with the same.

The Buddha taught his followers to cultivate an attitude of loving kindness towards each other and all living creatures. This attitude is summed up in the word metta, which means "goodwill" – to wish people well. The Buddha practised metta in his meetings with people:

Narrator: One day a rude and angry young man came up to the Buddha and started insulting him. The Buddha did not get upset. Instead, he asked the young man:

Buddha: If you buy a gift for someone, and that person does not take it, to whom does the gift belong?

Young Man: It would belong to me because I bought the gift.

Buddha: (smiling) That is right. And it is exactly the same with your anger. If you become angry with me and I do not get insulted, then the anger falls back on you. You are then the only one who becomes unhappy, not me. If you want to stop hurting yourself, you must get rid of your anger and become loving instead. When you hate others you yourself become unhappy.

The attitude of metta is likened to the sun. The sun radiates warmth and brightness which keep things alive and growing. If the sun went out, life would stop. So also if people live selfish lives they radiate no brightness to others, they become turned in on themselves. However, if people practise metta (goodwill towards others) their lives and others' become bright.

1 (a) What makes you angry?
(b) How do you react when you are angry – do you
  ▶ retaliate
  ▶ walk away from the situation
  ▶ try to understand why the person has made you angry
  ▶ have another reaction?
(c) Which do you think is the best reaction? Explain why.

2 (a) What do you think of the Buddha's response to the rude man?
(b) What do you think about his advice to the rude man – do you think it is good advice?

3 Imagine that you are a Buddhist. What would you say to your friend if he or she said to you: "If I'm always generous and forgive people they will take advantage of me"?

Right Speech

What is happening in this photograph?
▶ *Write a short story using the incident shown here.*
▶ *Discuss in what ways speech can be used for good and for bad.*

4 Do you ever lie? Is it ever right to lie? Is there a difference between a so-called "white lie" and an ordinary lie? What might a Buddhist say?

5 (a) Have you ever been hurt by words? What do you think of the old saying that "sticks and stones may break my bones but words can never hurt me"? Write of a time when you have either been hurt by words or helped (e.g. encouraged) by them.
(b) In groups discuss ways people at school use words to hurt others (e.g. name calling, verbal bullying). Why do they do it? What could be done about it?

RIGHT ACTION, LIVELIHOOD AND EFFORT

In this unit we will be exploring those parts of the Noble Eightfold Path concerned with morality: Right Action, Livelihood and Effort.

Right Action

Right action is summed up in the Five Precepts.

1 **First Precept** – I will not harm living beings.

> **1** (a) *Imagine you were the animals in this picture. Write a caption or bubble for each animal from the animal's point of view.*
> (b) *Do you have a pet at home? Discuss whether you think it is good for an animal to be a pet.*

Buddhists are to have an attitude of loving kindness towards all living beings: this includes people, animals, birds, insects, fish and sea creatures. For this reason Buddhists are often vegetarians.

Coffins

A can of sardines, tuna or sausages,
May often taste quite delicious,
But aren't you just prying open coffins
And feeding on stinking corpses?

> **2** (a) *Carry out a survey in your class to see how many people are vegetarian. What reasons do they give for being vegetarian?*
> (b) *What do you think of the poem "Coffins"? Do you agree with what it is saying?*
> (c) *Write a paragraph explaining why Buddhists are often vegetarian.*

2 **Second Precept** – I will not take what is not given.

3 **Third Precept** – I will avoid harmful sexual activity. One Buddhist explains this precept in the following way: "I am aware of the suffering caused by sexual misconduct. I am therefore determined not to engage in sexual relations without love and long-term commitment. I am determined to respect my commitments and the commitments of others. I will do everything in my power to protect children from sexual abuse and to prevent couples and families from being broken by sexual misconduct."

> **3** *Look through a teenage magazine. Make a list of the main topics covered. How many of the pages are concerned with sexual matters? What messages are these pages giving to you? Do you take much notice of what they say? Do you think it is a balanced message or do you think only one particular point of view is being given?*

4 **Fourth Precept** – I will avoid using words in incorrect ways (e.g. lying, gossiping, swearing, slander).

4 *Which of the Five Precepts do you think people in our society would find the hardest to keep? Say why. Try to follow the Fourth Precept for the following week. Keep a diary account of times when you tried hard to put it into practice and also times when you failed to keep it.*

5 **Fifth Precept** – I will not take drugs or drink that confuse the mind. Anything which clouds the mind stops a person from being aware and awake to the way things are.

▶ *This person is promising to tell the truth in a court of law while holding the Christian holy book, the Bible. What other occasions does the Fourth Precept apply to in everyday life?*

The precepts are seen as guidelines, as a way of training. Buddhists are not expected to be perfect all at once. It can take a long time to live up to them. In the Buddhist Scriptures it says: "Let a wise man remove impurities from himself even as a silversmith removes impurities from the silver: one after one, little by little, again and again." *(Dhammapada 239)*

Right Livelihood

5 *Taking on the precepts affects the way Buddhists choose their jobs. Visit the Careers Room. Make a list of jobs which a Buddhist could do. Make a list of jobs which a Buddhist could not do. Explain your choices.*

Right Effort

It takes effort and will-power to act in the right way. You need effort to be mindful of what you do, say and think. You need effort not to become attached to harmful thoughts and desires, and instead seek good thoughts.

▶ *Which of the jobs shown in the picture would a Buddhist not be able to do? Explain why.*

RIGHT AWARENESS

The final two steps of the Noble Eightfold Path are concerned with the mind, and we will explore these in this unit and unit 17. They are both concerned with meditation.

Our minds are often so busy asking a 101 questions such as "What am I going to do tonight?", "What does so and so think about me?" that they are rarely quiet and calm. One of the spokes of the Eightfold Wheel is Right Awareness (look back to page 29). The Buddha taught that we should wake up to the present — we are to see things as they are:

66 Our appointment with life is in the present moment. The place of our appointment is right here, in this very place. 99

Although it might sound odd, it is true that many of us do not live in the present. How many of you are reading this page and actually thinking about something else? For example, did you notice something odd about the clock face on this page?

One day a monk asked his master, "Where shall I look for Enlightenment?"
"Here."
"When will it happen?"
"It is happening right now."
"Then why don't I experience it?"
"Because you do not look."
"What should I look for?"
"Nothing. Just look."
"At what?"
"Anything your eyes alight upon."
"Must I look in a special kind of way?"
"No. The ordinary way will do."
"But don't I always look the ordinary way?"
"No."
"Why ever not?"
"Because to look you must be here. You're mostly somewhere else."

This Buddhist story explains the importance of Right Awareness:

One day two children were walking through a wood when they heard a strange sound. When they came around the corner they could see what was causing the noise – it was an ox-drawn cart with three men in it. One man was standing at the front holding out a telescope and looking ahead. The man at the back of the cart also had a telescope and was looking back at the way they had just come. Both had worried faces. The man in the middle was different – he seemed to be enjoying life. As the cart passed the children, the man in the middle called them to come into the cart. The other two men did not seem to notice them getting on the cart.

"What are they doing?" asked the children.

"Oh. All the one in the front knows how to do is to make plans and to worry about the future. All the one in the back knows how to do is to look behind him, to live in the past and regret everything he has done."

"What about you?" enquired the children.

"I look at the present – the here and now. The birds flying, the wind in the trees, the flowers flowering. Of course sometimes I look ahead to see where I am going and look back to see where I have come from, but the most important thing is to live in the present, because tomorrow has not yet arrived and yesterday has already gone. All that we have is now, the present."

1. (a) Who do you identify with in the story of the three men on the cart? Explain your response.
   (b) Do you ever lie awake at night worried what will happen the next day? What sort of things do you worry about?

2. Design a holiday called "Today's Day" to celebrate living in the present moment. What activities could you enjoy to celebrate the present? Make a poster or leaflet advertising the day.

3. (a) Go outside and sit quietly. What sounds of nature can you hear? Can you hear the birds singing? What does it sound like?
   (b) Look up into the night sky. What do you see? How many stars can you count? What does this make you feel?

RIGHT CONCENTRATION

In this unit you will consider the last step in the Noble Eightfold Path.

1 (a) What sort of things do you need to concentrate on? Do you find it easy to concentrate or does your mind flit from object to object? Explain your answer.

(b) Do you like silence or do you like to have music and/or the television as background noise? Why do you feel like this?

One way of thinking about our minds is to see them as pools of water, all stirred up and muddy with thoughts and feelings. When we feel like this we find it difficult to concentrate and be still. The point of meditation is first of all to let the mud settle so that we can look into the pool. Once our minds are still we can then look down and see what is at the bottom of the pool. The word "meditation" actually means clear seeing. Each day Buddhists practise meditation. It is a way of being calm and still. It demands concentration.

▶ What might this young Buddhist monk be feeling? Write a title for this photograph.

66 Our mind is out of control. It is just like a monkey jumping about senselessly. It goes upstairs, gets bored, runs back downstairs, gets tired of that, goes to the movie, gets bored again, has good food or poor food, gets bored with that to. 99
[Ajahn Chah, A Still Forest Pool]

2 Look at the description of the mind by Ajahn Chah. Do you think it is an accurate description of the way our minds work?

What is meditation?

One Buddhist described how he meditated in the following way:

66 The way you sit is very important. You need to keep your back straight so that you can breathe easily. It is best if you don't let your head droop down so that you slowly drowse off to sleep. Then close your eyes. Slowly concentrate on your breathing; become aware of what it feels like as it starts in your stomach, goes up through your chest and out of your mouth. Watch the breathing with your mind's eye. As you concentrate on your breathing you will become aware that it is not easy to be still – thoughts will come to your mind to distract you. Notice that thoughts are entering your mind but then return to your breathing. This form of meditation is called "**samatha**". It is concentration on an object like the breath. Use meditation to calm the heart and awaken the mind. 99

The pool in the photograph stands for the mind. The "strange and wonderful things" which come to the pool are our thoughts. In samatha meditation Buddhists become calm. Ajahn Chah said: "Once the mind is calm you can then investigate it. This is known as **vipassana** meditation. You can watch thoughts enter into your mind, examine them and then let them go. I find it useful to name what the distraction is in my mind and then to let go of it. Become aware of feelings arising and then passing away."

"Try to be mindful ... Then your mind will become still in any surroundings, like a clear forest pool. All kinds of wonderful, rare animals will come to drink at the pool, and you will clearly see the nature of all things. You will see many strange and wonderful things come and go, but you will be still ... This is the happiness of the Buddha.

(Ajahn Chah, A Still Forest Pool)

66 Meditation helps me to understand myself better – to make me look inside my mind to see what is there. 99
[Jessie, 14]

66 Meditation helps me to be calm, especially when I am feeling confused. 99
[Rosie, 14]

66 You have to keep practising meditation. At first it is as if we were young children trying to write the alphabet. The letters come out bent and sloppy, time and gain – the only thing to do is to keep at it. 99
[Mike, 16]

66 Man's inability to control and discipline his mind is responsible for all his problems. 99
[The Dalai Lama]

3 Draw a picture of your mind as a forest pool. What names would the "wonderful, rare animals" have who come to drink at the pool? Which are the nice animals? Which are the dangerous animals? Explain why.

4 Write a paragraph explaining what meditation is and why people meditate.

BEING REBORN

This unit looks at the Buddhist belief that people are reborn when they die.

Have you ever lived before? This may sound an odd question, but some people have experiences which make them believe that they have had previous lives. For example they go to a new place and suddenly feel they have been there before. This experience is called "déjà vu", which is French for "already seen".

Some people claim that under hypnosis they can remember events from previous lives.

The Buddha taught that people are caught in a cycle of birth, life, disease, old age, death and rebirth. This process of birth and rebirth is called **samsara**. The Buddha told a story about a burning house to explain this process of rebirth.

The burning house

In a certain village there was an old and very rich man who had a huge old house. Suddenly, the whole house was on fire. Now, that man, on seeing the house on fire, became alarmed and ran out of the house through the only door. But his children kept on playing inside, unaware of the flames licking around the house. The old man called to his children, but they wouldn't believe him, they weren't afraid, nor did they really understand what he meant by the words "burning" or "house".

[Based on the Lotus Sutra]

The Buddha taught that people are like the children in the story. He explained that to be in samsara is like being trapped in a burning house without even realising it. Inside the people are playing with the pleasures of the world unaware that the house is burning all around them. They do not seek a way out of the cycle of birth and rebirth.

(a) Why didn't the children take any notice of the old man?
(b) What are the pleasures and games that people become so attracted to in this world?
(c) What do you think the Buddha meant by "nor did they really understand what he meant by the words 'burning' or 'house'"?

Buddhists believe that people are reborn according to their **kamma**. The word means "action". It refers to the law of cause and effect. Good deeds bear good fruit, bad deeds bear bad fruit. They believe that the life or kammic energy of a person sets another life in motion. It is like the energy which is sent from one snooker ball to another.

2 *Do you think the law of kamma is fair? How might this law explain the fact that some people have to suffer more in this life than others?*

3 *Draw a diagram to illustrate the idea of rebirth. You could use the image of the billiard balls, or think up another way of showing energy passing from one object to another.*

Entering into Nibbana

The aim of the Buddhist life is to become free of the cycle of samsara (or birth and rebirth) and to enter into Nibbana. The word "Nibbana" means "blown out" – the image being that of a flame which is blown out. The message of Buddhism is like a fire alarm – to wake people up to the fact that "all is burning" with the fires of desire (greed, hatred and ignorance). When these fires are blown out the suffering of rebirth is at an end and there is Nibbana.

Nibbana is a very difficult thing to describe. A Zen teacher, Thich Nhat Hanh, describes Nibbana in the following way:

> ❝ There are two dimensions to life, and we should be able to touch both. One is like a wave, and we call it the historical dimension. The other is like the water, and we call it the ultimate dimension, or Nibbana. We usually touch just the wave. In the historical dimension, we have birth certificates and death certificates. This is the world of waves. It is characterised by birth and death, ups and downs. A wave has a beginning and an end, but water does not have these characteristics. In the world of water, there is no birth or death, no beginning or end. When we touch the water, we touch reality in its ultimate dimension and are made free. ❞

NINETEEN

THE WHEEL OF LIFE

This unit examines the six realms into which people are reborn.

If you had to draw a picture of the inside of your mind what would you draw? The Tibetan Buddhist Wheel of Life is like a map of the mind. It contains six realms. Buddhists use it as a mirror in which their minds are reflected. It also describes the six realms into which people are reborn. The realms stand for types of being rather than actual places. Read what each of the realms stands for and see whether you recognise something of yourself in each one.

The six realms

1 The heavenly realm

▶ Have you ever felt totally happy? What does it feel like? What makes you feel like this?

▶ Look at this realm. How is pleasure shown?

This realm is about pleasure – life is one big party. In this realm people spend their days gaping at beautiful sights. However, this realm doesn't last for ever – that's the thing people in this realm forget while they are having so much fun.

2 The power seekers' realm

▶ What is happening in this realm? What feelings do you think people have in this realm? Why are there castles – what do you think they stand for? Why is a man trying to axe down the tree?

3 The animal realm

▶ What do you think it is like to be an animal? What feelings do you think animals have? What makes them act in the way they do? Why do you think there is a picture of the Buddha reading a book in this realm?

The animal realm stands for those who act on blind instinct; people who do whatever they feel like doing without carefully thinking about their actions.

4 The hell realm

▶ What do people mean when they say that they are "going through hell at the moment"? Describe a situation in which people would use this term. What feelings do people have in this realm?

▶ Have you ever been bullied? Have you ever been so angry with someone that you really wanted to hurt them? Have you ever been so frightened that you couldn't even move? This is the most painful realm to be in.

5 The hungry ghost realm

▶ Look carefully at the hungry ghosts. Why do you think they have thin necks and bloated stomachs? What is the picture saying?

Ghosts in this realm are always being greedy. They are always craving for something to fill their huge stomachs, but it never seems to be enough. Their tiny necks can never take in enough food to satisfy them.

6 The human realm

▶ Carefully look at what is happening in this realm. Then write a description of it by completing the sentence: Human life is about …

1 *Use newspapers and magazines to make up a collage to illustrate the six realms. Select a picture and/or article for each realm.*

2 *Imagine that it is Saturday morning and you are in town waiting in a bus queue to catch a bus home. There are six other people in the queue. You can already tell several things about the people if you watch carefully. As you watch, try writing a poem called "Faces in the Crowd" in which you show how the six people each reflect one of the six realms of life.*

3 *Write a detailed diary for one day. Include what you do, how you feel, what thoughts you have. How many different realms do you inhabit during one day?*

TWENTY

MONKS AND NUNS

The Buddha taught his followers for forty-five years before he died. During the rainy season they gathered together and formed the **Sangha** (community of monks). The settlements where they rested were known as **viharas** (resting places). The Buddhist Sangha today is made up of monks (called **bhikkhus**) and nuns (called **bhikkhunis**). Some Sanghas also include the laypeople.

Like the Buddha himself, monks and nuns own only that which is essential: an alms bowl, a razor, a needle, a toothpick, an outer robe, an under robe and a cloak. A Buddhist explained: "The robe is a symbol of renouncing luxury. It is cut and sewn to resemble patchwork, because the original robes were made from scrap rags." Theravada monks wear saffron robes, Tibetan monks wear maroon robes and Zen monks wear black robes. (You will find out about these different varieties of Buddhism on pages 46–49.) The Buddha established a code for monks to live by. This code is called the **Vinaya**.

Each monk and nun owns an alms bowl. The word "alms" means gift or donation. The word "bhikkhu" means one who lives on alms. Every morning these monks in Thailand will collect their daily food from the local Buddhist community. They are not allowed to ask for food though – it has to be freely offered. This is the main meal of the day for monks and is to be eaten before noon.

1 *Explain the following words: Sangha, bhikkhu, bhikkhuni, vihara, alms.*

Daily life in a Theravada monastery in England

4.30	Monks are woken by the rising bell
5.00	Meditation session
7.15	Breakfast and house meeting to discuss work projects for the day
8.30	Alms round
11.00	Return to the monastery to eat the main meal of the day
1.00	Work or study period
5.00	Afternoon tea – which provides an opportunity for lay Buddhists to receive teaching from the monks
7.30	Chanting and meditation session
9.30	To bed

Why become a monk?

In Buddhism you can stop being a monk or nun at any time – it is not a lifelong commitment, though many do stay all their lives and this is encouraged. Alan explains why he became a monk:

2 ▸ *Monks and nuns live a simple life, owning little. Imagine that you are going to join a monastery and you are only allowed three items in your suitcase. What would you take? Why?*

❝ Like most parents my parents wanted me to be successful, get married, have children and lead a pretty normal life. And I've had a good try. However, I kept having this feeling that I wanted to find something really worthwhile. At university I studied psychology because I wanted to understand myself and other people better. Just after completing my degree I went on a ten-day meditation course. The entire ten-day period was in silence. During the ten days I was introduced to Buddhist teachings and started to observe something that was happening to me – that when desires arose in me they also passed away.

In the past I had thought that there were only two ways of treating desires: either to give in to them and get what I wanted (this pleased me for a short time until I got fed up with it and wanted something else), or I didn't follow my desires and got frustrated. Now I was almost shaking with the desire to get up and leave. But as I sat still with the desire I watched it die and pass away. Each time it passed I would just feel so incredibly peaceful. I no longer had to give in to every desire or feel frustrated if my desires were not met. ❞

3 ▸ *(a) Why did Alan decide to stay in the monastery and become a monk?*
(b) By yourself try to sit still for an hour. What thoughts and feelings did you have? How did you manage to keep still? What qualities do you think Alan must have?

4 ▸ *What questions would you like to ask a Buddhist monk or nun? As a class discuss what their answers might be. Give your reasons.*

Meditation is at the heart of life in a monastery.

LAY BUDDHISTS

This unit explores the relationship of the Sangha to lay people.

The Sangha is a two-way community between the monks and nuns and the lay Buddhists. Michael is a lay Buddhist. He describes what the relationship with the monks and nuns is like:

> ❝ Going to the vihara gives me space to think and be still – to let my mind calm down and to start to see things clearly. This is important since I live a very busy life. In return I recognise the importance of the monks and nuns to me by taking them food – I give them the things they need for their bodies to live; they give me what I need for my inside life to live. ❞

A monk teaching a lay Buddhist in Wimbledon.

The vihara, or monastery, is the centre of community life for Buddhists. Lay Buddhists often come to the monastery at major turning-points in life – for example, at the birth of a new baby, when two people get married, at the death of a loved one – and also to celebrate Buddhist festivals (see pages 60–1). On each occasion they will bring gifts or robes and food for the monks and nuns, and in return they will receive teaching (Dhamma) from the ordained community.

In Britain, Sunday is a good day for families to come to monasteries. Some monasteries organize summer camps where Buddhist families come from all over the country to get to know each other and receive the Dhamma from the monks. It is also a time to practise meditation.

When lay Buddhists go and stay in a monastery for a few days they follow all of the Ten Precepts, the five discussed on pages 32–3 and five more, where people undertake:

6 not to eat after midday
7 not to be involved in dancing, acting or music
8 not to wear jewellery or perfume
9 not to sleep in a soft bed
10 not to handle money.

"We could go to somewhere like Majorca in the summer, but I think this is better. There's more quality in it. At the end of one of the summer camps you get a really good feeling from it. It's like a family – all around there's the loving kindness, and you get a feeling from that."

1 ▶ (a) If you were to go and stay in a monastery for a few days which of the last five precepts would you find most difficult to keep? Explain why.
(b) Why do you think the Buddha advised his monks to keep these precepts – what is their value?

2 ▶ Design a leaflet for a Buddhist monastery which would help a visitor understand life there.

3 ▶ Imagine you are spending your summer holiday at a Buddhist summer camp in Britain. Write a diary entry, or short story, or a letter to a friend about your experiences. (Remember that you will have to follow the last five precepts during your stay.)

THERAVADA AND MAHAYANA BUDDHISM

By the time the Buddha died, he had thousands of followers in India. During the next few centuries, Buddhism spread through Asia. In the next three units we will look at the different varieties of Buddhism found in the world today. This unit will look at Theravada and Mahayana Buddhism.

Emperor Ashoka

The person who was responsible for Buddhism becoming a world religion was Emperor Ashoka. He inherited an Indian empire in about 270 BCE and, like most rulers, used violence to conquer his enemies. However, after one campaign he appears to have had a religious conversion. He was sickened by all his violence and bloodshed. He gave up warfare and became a Buddhist. He began to rule his empire according to Buddhist teachings and became the first Buddhist ruler. He built hospitals and stopped the killing of animals for food. He sent missionaries to other countries to spread Buddhism, and sent his son and daughter to Sri Lanka, where the king was converted to Buddhism.

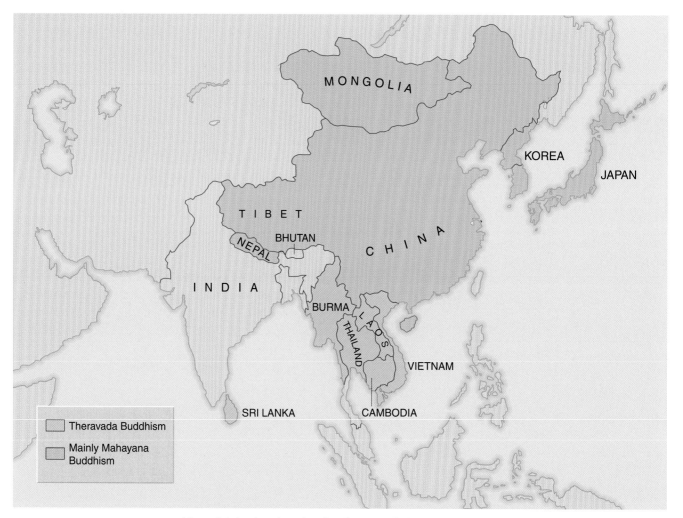

Map of Asia showing the distribution of Theravada and Mahayana Buddhism.

Two schools of Buddhism

After the Buddha's death in about 480 BCE, a council made up of the Buddha's closest followers met at Rajgir in northern India. The aim was to agree on the exact words of the Buddha, which were to be handed down from memory. However, about a hundred years later there was a second council at which people disagreed on how to interpret the Buddha's teaching. Those who accepted the interpretation of this council became known as the Elders. Those who disagreed left the council. From this split gradually arose the two main schools of Buddhism – **Theravada** (the Way of the Elders) and **Mahayana** (the Great Vehicle). Although both schools hold to the main teachings of Buddhism, they practise their faith in different ways. Today, both types of Buddhism are represented in Britain.

Theravada Buddhism

One modern Buddhist said: "The main claim of Theravada Buddhism is that it represents the original teaching of the Buddha, and what appeals to me about it is its simplicity." Traditionally, Theravada Buddhists follow the example of the Buddha in living simple lives of meditation in remote forests. In Theravada countries it is possible to see monks going on their alms round just after dawn to give the laypeople an opportunity to offer them food. In Burma it is estimated that the average Burmese man spends a quarter of his salary supporting the monks. It is often said that "To be a Burmese is to be a Buddhist." In Burma, the Buddha, the Dhamma and the Sangha are highly respected by everyone. In Thailand, about a quarter of a million men join the Sangha and go on Rains Retreat every year.

Mahayana Buddhism

As Buddhism spread through different countries it adapted to the cultures of the people. There are therefore a number of different forms of Mahayana Buddhism, such as Tibetan and Zen Buddhism (see unit 23). One difference between Theravada and Mahayana Buddhists is in the Mahayana belief about the bodhisattva. Bodhisattvas are wise beings who only think of the good of others. They are so kind that they decide not to leave the world at death but keep coming back to earth to help others.

1. ▶ *Why do you think that Burmese men give so much money to the monks each year? What does this tell you about the relationship between the monks and the lay Buddhists?*

2. ▶ *Do you think it is a good thing that men join the Sangha for a time? What do you think the King of Thailand would have learnt when he entered the monastery for a short time?*

3. ▶ *Collect travel brochures about Burma, Sri Lanka and Thailand. Do they mention Buddhism? If so, what do you learn about Buddhism from them? Do travel brochures of England mention religion? What do your findings tell you about England?*

▶ *This picture shows a bodhisattva (Avalokitesvara). Draw your own image of loving kindness and compassion. Give it a label explaining what you have drawn.*

TIBETAN AND ZEN BUDDHISM

In this unit we look at Tibetan Buddhism and Zen Buddhism.

Tibetan Buddhism

Buddhism was introduced to Tibet from India in the seventh century CE. Before the Chinese invaded Tibet in the 1950s there were over 6000 monasteries. Today, however, many of the monasteries have been destroyed and some 100,000 Tibetan Buddhists have left their country, many escaping across the border into India. Tibetan Buddhism is fighting for survival.

Tibetan Buddhism is very distinctive and colourful: it encourages people to get involved in religion with their feelings as well as their minds. Shrine rooms are heavily decorated with wall hangings, called thangkas.

There are many rituals, such as the use of prayer wheels and prayer flags. During festivals long horns are blown and there is much dancing. Tibetan Buddhists refer to a religious leader or teacher as a "lama". The relationship between the teacher and the pupil is a very important one and this is reflected in the fact that Tibetan Buddhists add a fourth refuge or jewel to the traditional three: "I go to the lama for refuge." The most senior teacher is called the Dalai Lama.

The Dalai Lama

1 *Make a list of occasions when people use flags. What do people use flags for, why are they important? How do Tibetan Buddhists use flags? What do you think Tibetan Buddhists might think when they see a prayer flag?*

Tibetan prayer flags. Prayers written on the flags are carried by the wind.

Zen Buddhism

Buddhism first came to Japan from Korea in the sixth century CE. The sect of Zen Buddhism began in China and took root in Japan around the year 1200. "Zen" means meditation, and indicates the importance which this school of Buddhism places on meditation practice. "Buddha's teaching must be performed in our daily lives." (The Abbot of Eiheiji Monastery)

In a Zen monastery the most important room is the zendo, which is the meditation hall. However, it is also the place where the monks eat and sleep. All of life's activities form part of the monk's meditation practice. Every activity must be carried out with concentration and mindfulness.

In the same way Zen Buddhism uses activities such as archery, judo and swordsmanship as a way of disciplining the body and mind to work together, to become calm.

One of the two schools of Zen Buddhism, Rinzai, stresses the importance of the relationship between the Zen master and pupil. The master uses word puzzles (called koans) as a way of waking up the mind. They cannot be answered by the ordinary mind. Instead, they encourage reflection and take the person beyond the limits of the intellect towards Enlightenment. Perhaps the most famous of these is: "If clapping two hands produces sound, what is the sound of one hand clapping?" There are about 1700 koans altogether.

Monks at the Soto Zen monastery Eiheiji in central Japan. All of life's activities are made into a ritual and become part of meditation practice.

Buddhists in Japan observing the tea ceremony, in which the simple activity of taking tea is made into a ritual which encourages concentration. Taking tea can therefore become a way of calming and developing the mind.

2 ▶ *Write a sentence on each of the following: Zen, zendo, koan.*

3 ▶ (a) *Look at the pictures on this page. What feelings come to mind when you look at them and read the captions?*

(b) *How does the Zen Buddhists' way of drinking tea or working differ from the way you do these things?*

BUDDHISM SPREADS TO THE WEST

In this unit we look at the recent spread of Buddhism in the West.

In the last thirty years Buddhism has spread greatly in the West. Because of travel, Buddhist teachings have become more available and people are starting to find out more about the religion. Also some people in the West who are caught up in the world of work and making money are becoming attracted to a different way of seeing things. They are looking for ways to understand themselves and the world they live in better, and are attracted to the practice of meditation as present in Theravada, Zen and Tibetan Buddhism.

In addition to these older schools of Buddhism there are new orders such as the Friends of the Western Buddhist Order, which adapts the teachings of Buddhism to people in the West. "Friends" are not monks. They run centres where people can come and learn meditation.

According to the Buddhist Directory there are over 270 Buddhist groups and centres in the UK and Ireland. This map shows where they are. Some places have more than one centre. The directory is published by the Buddhist Society in London.

People in Britain who were not brought up in Buddhist families are turning to Buddhism for a number of reasons:

66 Buddhism could be described as a "try-it-and see" religion. You don't have to believe a lot of things before you can be a Buddhist. Instead, the Buddha taught that you should try out his teachings and see if they are relevant to your life. 99
[Peggy]

I was attracted by Buddhist teachings about compassion for all living things. This teaching is so important at a time when we are in danger of destroying animal and plant life and even threatening to destroy the world by pollution. 99
[Emily]

Each of these photos shows Buddhists in Britain

1 *Write a paragraph explaining why you think Buddhism is becoming popular in Britain.*

2 *What difficulties might Buddhists have living in Britain? Look back at the Five Precepts which all Buddhists have to keep (pages 32–3).*

TWENTY-FIVE

THE THREE BASKETS

This unit describes the Buddhist Scriptures.

> **1** *Ask your parents or grandparents to tell you stories about their parents. Write them down. Start collecting your own family stories that have been passed down by word of mouth.*

For about 400 years the Buddha's teachings were passed on orally, by word of mouth. The first Buddhist Scriptures were written down by Theravada monks in the Pali language (a language similar to the one spoken by the Buddha). There is a legend that they were written on palm leaves and stored in three baskets. This collection became known as the Pali canon, or **Tipitaka** (ti-pitaka = three baskets). The Pali canon consists of three sections or "baskets".

The Buddhist scriptures being studied in a Burmese monastery.

1 Vinaya Pitaka

This "basket" or section contains the 227 rules that monks and nuns have to follow. It covers what they can possess and how they should act.

2 Sutta Pitaka

This "basket" contains the teachings of the Buddha. The word "sutta" means thread or topic. The suttas are discourses or conversations, often between the Buddha and a follower. The Sutta Pitaka is subdivided into five Nikayas, or collections. (The stories of the arrow and of the raft on pages 14 and 28 come from two of these Nikayas.)

The Sutta Pitaka contains the Four Noble Truths and the Noble Eightfold Path, as well as a collection of the Buddha's sayings known as the *Dhammapada*. It also contains Jataka tales. These are stories about the Buddha's previous lives. They are tales which show how the Buddha lived out the ten qualities (or perfections) which lead to buddhahood: generosity, virtue, renunciation, wisdom, energy, patience, truthfulness, resolution, loving kindness and an even temper. They encourage people to live out these qualities too. "The noble horse" is one of these stories.

The noble horse

The King of Benares had the most beautiful horse in the world: he was as swift as a deer and as graceful as a swan. At that time, Benares was a strong and happy kingdom, so much so that seven other kings felt threatened by its power. They gathered their armies and marched against Benares.

The King of Benares called one of his knights and asked what chance they had. The knight replied, "We can succeed, but only if you allow me to ride your favourite horse."

As the knight rushed into battle, he defeated the first six kings one after the other. They were all taken prisoner. But in capturing the sixth king, the horse was wounded and had to be taken to the stables. The knight called for another horse. As the knight was about to mount, his wounded horse thought: "On another horse, my brave rider will be killed." And, calling the knight, the horse spoke to him and persuaded him to take him back into battle.

The knight rode the horse into battle, defeated the seventh king and brought him back a prisoner. But when the battle was over, the horse fell bleeding to the ground. The king knelt at his side, and a soft whisper came from the horse's lips: "Be not sad, my king," he said, "my wounds do not pain me, for the victory is won. But do not slay those who are now your prisoners. Let them return to their homes promising never to attack Benares again." Then the great one closed his eyes and died. The seven kings were released, and war never broke out again. The people of all the kingdoms loved one another.

> **2** What qualities is the story of the noble horse encouraging?

> **3** Choose one of the Ten Perfections. Write your own Jataka tale as a children's story, encouraging people to practise that quality. Illustrate it.

3 Abhidhamma Pitaka

The third "basket" contains discussions on how to understand and interpret the Buddha's teachings.

Mahayana Buddhists have many other Scriptures. Some of these are called "sutras", which is the word "sutta" in the Sanskrit language.

TWENTY-SIX

BUDDHIST PRACTICES

1 *Who do you respect? What do you do to show your respect to them? If you wanted to give that person a gift, what would you give them? Explain your choice.*

Buddhists do not worship the Buddha as a god. Instead they show respect to the Buddha's teaching and to what the Buddha points to – the state of Enlightenment. Buddhists often show their respect by bringing offerings to a shrine or temple, and placing them in front of an image of the Buddha. They may bring:

▶ flowers – which today are fresh but will fade and die, just like our bodies

▶ light (candles or butter lamps) – which give light just as the Buddha's teachings give light and truth

▶ incense – which is a sign of the sweet fragrance of the Buddha's teaching.

Mahayana Buddhists may offer the seven gifts that would be offered to an honoured guest after a long journey: water for drinking, water for washing feet, flowers, incense, light, perfumed water for a bath, food. They can all be symbolised by a bowl of water in front of the shrine.

The Erewan Shrine in Thailand

Meditation is at the centre of Buddhist practice. Buddhists use different aids to help them to meditate.

This is the Rinzai Zen garden in Japan. The gravel is raked to form careful patterns. It is used by Zen Buddhists to help them meditate. This garden is unchanging – there are no flowers that fade or leaves that fall. The only changes that happen occur in how a person looks at it. Zen gardens can be made up of sand or gravel, water, rocks, mosses and sometimes a tree.

2 (a) How might a Zen garden help Buddhists become calm and meditate?
(b) Design a Zen garden using the elements listed above. Think how you are going to encourage feelings of peace and calm that would help a person to meditate. You could do a small version of it on a tray.

3 Some Buddhists will chant a mantra to help them concentrate.
(a) At what occasions do people chant (e.g. at a football match)? What do they chant? Why do they chant?
(b) Why do you think particular words or sounds have power when they are repeated over and over again?

This is a small section of a mandala (a sacred design within a "circle"). Mandalas are used by Tibetan Buddhists for meditation. They are sometimes made of coloured sand. The Tibetan monks start with a central design and then work outwards on a spiritual journey.

A Tibetan Buddhist spinning a prayer wheel. Buddhists sometimes write a mantra on a piece of paper and place it in the prayer wheel. A mantra is a religious phrase that is chanted over and over again. By turning the prayer wheel the spiritual power of the mantra is released into the world.

TWENTY-SEVEN

GROWING UP AS A BUDDHIST

How do you think good parents should bring up their children? What qualities do you think are important for them to teach? Are there particular experiences which you think parents should give their children? This unit examines how Buddhists bring up their children and how they mark the different stages of life.

Birth

Buddhists do not have special ceremonies to celebrate the birth of a child since they believe that this is not a new birth but a rebirth from a previous existence. However, parents can take their babies to the Sangha and request a name with a special meaning for their child. Buddhist parents attempt to bring up their children to follow the Buddha's teachings. In some countries, monasteries will contain a school where the children are educated. In addition, they provide classes for those who wish to become monks and nuns.

1 (a) When people celebrate stages in life they are celebrating a rite of passage – a passage from one stage of life to another. Do you think it is important to mark the birth of a child with such a ceremony? If so, what do you think should be the ceremony?

(b) Why don't Buddhists have ceremonies to mark the birth of a child?

(c) Do you know what your name means? Look it up in a dictionary of names if you can. What do you think is the purpose of giving a child a name with a special meaning?

A class in the Sangha in Thailand

Initiation

In some countries sons will leave their families and spend a period of time in the Sangha in order to learn meditation and receive teaching. This can happen at the end of schooling and before the son goes on to university or a job. It is thought to be a good training for life. The present King of Thailand became a monk for a short time.

The young boy in Burma will arrive at the Sangha dressed in rich clothes. He will then exchange them for a simple robe in imitation of the Buddha who gave up the rich life of the palace for that of wandering holy man. He will have his head shaved as the Buddha did when he went into the forest to search for happiness. The boy will then make a promise to the senior monk to follow the rules of the Sangha and the teachings of the Buddha.

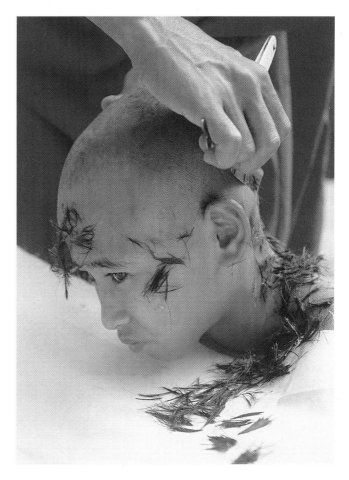

Marriage

Although Buddhists think family life and the way you bring up your children is very important, they don't have any special ceremonies for marriage. Buddhists usually follow local wedding customs.

In Buddhism, women and men are equally important. They both have the responsibility of taking on the Three Refuges and bringing up children according to the Five Precepts and the teachings of the Buddha. Generosity is a very important virtue in Buddhism. Parents will bring their children to the Sangha to offer dana meals. They prepare the meals for the monks and nuns, as well as providing other essential items like medicine. Families are always welcome at the monastery; some even invite families to stay overnight and on retreat. Buddhist families may also set up a shrine in a room at home. On the shrine there will be a statue of the Buddha and offerings of candles, incense and fresh flowers. Families will chant and meditate in front of the shrine.

2 *(a) Do you think that the education system you are in is good? If you could design your own education, what things do you think it would be important to include?*

(b) Do you think it is a good thing for children to spend time away from their parents? What can be the advantages? What do you think of the Buddhist tradition of children spending some time in a monastery? What could the advantages be?

3 *Give each of the photographs on these two pages a title that describes what is happening in the photograph. Choose one photograph and write down a question which you would like to ask a person in it.*

ACCEPTING DEATH

This unit examines the Buddhist attitude towards death, and asks you to consider your own attitude towards death.

1. (a) What do you think about death? Are you frightened of it or do you think it is something to be looked forward to?
   (b) Have you ever been to a funeral? If so, what stuck in your memory? What feelings did you have?

The Buddha taught that death is not something to be feared. It is just a stepping stone on the journey towards Nibbana. We have already seen that Buddhists do not believe that death is the end – they believe in rebirth. Therefore, although Buddhists are naturally sad to say goodbye to a friend or relative, they are also happy for them. Buddhist ceremonies for the dead are occasions for reflecting on the teachings of impermanence. Death is an important part of life for Buddhists, an opportunity to grieve and think about their own mortality.

Buddhists teach that it helps to have a right attitude about our deaths. They try to cultivate a balanced attitude towards death. The positive attitude is to accept it. One Buddhist told the following story to illustrate this point:

A procession to a cremation in Bali.

66 Suppose you're about to travel on the train from London to Edinburgh. You get on the train and think: "This is very nice, I think I'll stay here for ever!" You put your name over the carriage; put curtains up in your compartment and think, "Quite a nice little home." Then you get to Edinburgh and the porter comes on and tells you to get off. But you're clinging to the seat saying, "I don't want to get off, this compartment's so nice."

If someone behaved like that you'd think they were insane. But if you think about it, our normal attitude to life is equally insane, equally bizarre – we fight death and hold on to life. To develop a positive attitude towards death you need to admit from the beginning that you've got to get off again at some point. While I'm here I can enjoy the carriage, this body; but I must not cling too tightly, because one day I will have to give it up. 99

Monks have an active part to play in the death rites since it is an occasion for teaching. When a Buddhist dies, the body is washed and laid in a wooden coffin. The coffin is sometimes taken to a monastery, and the body is usually cremated and the ashes collected. A monk will deliver a sermon such as the following, which draws attention to the impermanence of life:

> 66 When one does not understand death, life can be very confusing. If our body really belonged to us, it would obey our commands. If we say, "Don't get old," or "I forbid you to get sick," does it obey us? No, it takes no notice. We only rent this house, not own it. If we think it belongs to us, we will suffer when we have to leave it. But, in reality, there is nothing solid or unchanging that we can hold on to. 99
>
> [Ajahn Chah, A Still Forest Pool]

Look at this photo of a monk meditating in Sri Lanka.
▶ Why do you think he is doing this?
▶ What do you think is going through his mind?
▶ What do you think about him doing this?
▶ Do you think he has a healthy attitude to death?

2 ▶ Reread the Buddhist story of the London–Edinburgh train. In what ways do people cling on to life? What things do they cling on to in life? Why do you think some people are afraid of death and resist it like the person who would not get out of the carriage?

3 ▶ What do you think Ajahn Chah meant when he said "We only rent this house, not own it"? How do you think this affects the way he lives life?

4 ▶ If you had to design a ceremony to mark the death of a loved one, what would you include? What atmosphere do you think would be important?

5 ▶ Use teaching on impermanence (pages 18–19) to write a sermon that a Buddhist monk might give at a funeral. How could you use the story of Kisa Gotami and the mustard seed (see page 21) in your sermon?

TWENTY-NINE

CELEBRATING FESTIVALS

Which festivals do you celebrate? Which do you enjoy the most? Do you think it is important to have festivals during the year? In this unit you will be looking at Buddhist festivals and what role they play in the lives of Buddhists.

Buddhist festivals are times for joy. They give Buddhists opportunities to meet together, to say the Three Refuges and learn more about the Buddha's teaching. Families bring food, candles and flowers to the monks in the monasteries. In return, the monks chant scriptures appropriate to the festival, lead a period of meditation and provide teaching on the themes of the festival. All the important festivals take place at the time of the full moon. The festivals are different in different Buddhist traditions.

Wesak (Buddha Day)

This Theravada festival celebrates three major events in the life of the Buddha: his birth, Enlightenment and death. It is the most important festival and is celebrated in different ways in Sri Lanka, Burma and Thailand. In Britain, Buddhists send Wesak cards to each other. These will be decorated with symbols representing the Buddha's birth and Enlightenment, such as the lotus flower (standing for purity and Enlightenment), or the Bodhi tree. In Mahayana countries, the birth, Enlightenment and death of the Buddha are celebrated on different days.

The following account of the Buddha's Enlightenment gives a flavour of the atmosphere of the festival of Wesak. In it Mara, the evil one, has been defeated.

> And the moon, like a maiden's gentle smile, lit up the heavens, while a rain of sweet-scented flowers, filled with moisture, fell down to earth from above.
> … and the leader of all reached the state of all-knowledge … the earth swayed like a woman drunken with wine, the sky shone bright … and the mighty drums of thunder resounded through the air … At that moment no one anywhere was angry, ill, or sad … the world became quite quiet, as though it had reached full perfection.
>
> [Buddhacarita]

1 Make your own lanterns and cards for Wesak. Decorate them with symbols of the Buddha's birth and Enlightenment such as lotus flowers, lights and the Bodhi tree.

2 Buddhists use light (candles, butter lamps) to celebrate Wesak to recall that the Buddha showed people how to become enlightened. Read the account of the Buddha's Enlightenment (Unit 5). Why do you think lights are such powerful symbols?

Wesak being celebrated in Thailand. There is a party feel to the whole occasion. Houses and streets are cleaned and decorated with flags and flowers. In villages, Buddhists gather around statues of the Buddha when it is dark. They walk around the statue with candles till all is covered in light.

▶ *Write a short speech that a Buddhist monk might give at the festival. Use this unit and Units 2 to 5 to help you.*

The Kathina festival

During the lifetime of the Buddha, his wandering monks were criticised by farmers for walking through their flooded fields and thus destroying the crops. The Buddha therefore told his monks to stay in one place during the three months of the rainy season. This time is called the Rainy Season Retreat (Vassa). The beginning and the end of the Retreat are marked by festivals.

The day before the Retreat begins is called Asahla-Puja. It celebrates the Buddha's first sermon. The Retreat comes to an end with the Kathina ceremony in which lay Buddhists bring cloth to make new robes for the monks. The monks sew some of the cloth into a robe before dawn of the next day. This robe is then offered to a chosen senior monk.

3 *Have you ever received a gift from someone which is really precious, even though it might not be worth much in money? What makes it precious?*

4 *In Buddhist countries, festivals take place throughout the year. Choose one of the following festivals: the Festival of the Tooth Relic in Sri Lanka; New Year festival; Loy Krthong; Losar (Tibetan festival); Obon (Japanese festival). Use books in your library to find out what it celebrates and how people celebrate it. What is the mood of the festival? Present your research as a poster, display, a talk to your class or a children's book.*

GLOSSARY

Anatta   People have no permanent self or soul

Anicca   Everything changes, nothing lasts for ever

Bhikkhu (m) **Bhikkhuni** (f)   Buddhist monk or nun

Bodhisattva   A person who has attained Enlightenment but comes back to earth to help others

Buddha   An awakened or enlightened one; Siddattha Gotama

Buddha rupa   A statue of the Buddha

Dalai Lama   Leader of Tibetan Buddhists

Dana   "Giving"; the daily meal of Theravada Buddhists

Dhamma   (in Sanskrit: Dharma) The teaching of the Buddha

Dukkha   Second Mark of Life and First Noble Truth: life is unsatisfactory

Enlightenment   The state of full understanding about the way things are in life

Jataka Tales   Stories of the previous lives of the Buddha

Kamma   "Action"; it refers to intentional action and to the law of cause and effect

Koan   Word puzzle used to create awareness in Zen Buddhism

Lama   "Teacher" in Tibetan Buddhism

Lay Buddhists   Buddhists who are not ordained monks or nuns

Lotus   The lotus flower is a symbol of Enlightenment

Mahayana   One of the two main schools of Buddhism; the Northern School

Mandala   "Circle"; pictorial diagram used in meditation

Mantra   Set of words or sounds that have a religious significance when repeated

Mara   The evil one in Buddhism

Marks of Life, Three,   Three aspects of unsatisfactoriness in life: Anicca, Dukkha, Anatta

Meditation   "Clear seeing"; mental training that leads to Enlightenment

Metta   "Loving kindness"; compassion towards others, wishing others well

Nibbana   (in Sanskrit: Nirvana) "Extinguished" or "blown out"; refers to the state of being set free from the endless cycle of birth and rebirth, a state of perfect peace

Noble Eightfold Path   The Fourth Noble Truth: the cure for ending Dukkha; also referred to as the Middle Way

Noble Truths, Four,   Main Buddhist teachings about the nature of suffering, the cause of suffering and the way to end suffering

Precepts   Guidelines for conduct: ordained monks and nuns follow the Ten Precepts; lay Buddhists normally follow just Five Precepts

Rebirth   Belief that a person has other lives before and after this one

Refuges, Three,   (or Three Jewels) The three most precious things in Buddhism: the Buddha, the Dhamma, the Sangha

Samatha   A form of meditation in which you concentrate on an object (e.g. breath) in order to become calm and still

Samsara   Endless cycle of birth, death and rebirth

Sangha   "Community"; in Theravada countries it refers to Buddhist monks and nuns; sometimes includes laypeople as well

Sutta   "Thread", "topic" or "single idea"; refers to Buddhist religious texts

Tanha   "Thirst": craving or desire

Thangka   Hanging religious picture

Theravada   One of the two main schools of Buddhism; Southern School

Tipitaka   The three "baskets" containing the holy books of the Pali canon of Buddhist Scripture

Vihara   "Resting place"; Buddhist temple or monastery

Vinaya   Discipline, rules of life, the 227 rules of Theravada monks

Vipassana   Insight meditation

Wesak   Festival celebrating the Buddha's birth, Enlightenment and death

Zen   School of Buddhism that developed in Japan

Zendo   Meditation room in Zen Buddhism

INDEX

ACKNOWLEDGEMENTS

The author would like to thank the Venerable Kusalo and Peggy Morgan for helpful suggestions during the preparation of the book for publication. The author and publishers would also like to thank the following for permission to reproduce photographs:

The Bridgeman Art Library London p1 (Christie's London), p23 (British Museum, London); Bubbles p31 (Loisjoy Thurston); Bruce Coleman Ltd p19 top (P Clement); Collections p22 (Brian Shuel); The Dharma School p45; Peter Douglas p47; Eye Ubiquitous p7 (Tim Page), 55 right (Bennett Dean), 58 (Simon Arnold); Robert Harding Picture Library p54 (Ken Wilson), 57; Graham Harrison pp36, 42, 43, 48 bottom, 49 right, 51 top, 52, 59; Michael Holford p11 (Musée Guimet), 15 (British Museum); Peter Wren Howard p40; Hulton Getty p8 left; Hutchison Library p8 right, p55 top (P. Goycoolea); Kagyu Samyé-Ling p51 bottom; Magnum Photos p9 top (Raghu Rai), p10 (Abbas), p17 Marilyn Silverstone); David Muscroft Picture Library p39; NHPA p19 centre and bottom (Stephen Dalton), p37 David Woodfall; Christine Osborne Pictures p56; © Ann and Bury Peerless-Slide Resources and Picture Library p16; Rex Features Ltd p21 (Tom Haley), p33 (Chat Magazine); Science Photo Library p38 (Francoise Sauze); John Bigelow Taylor p55 bottom; Trip p9 bottom (H. Rogers), p13 (H. Rogers), p44 (H Rogers), p48 top (T. Noorits); Zefa Pictures pp4, 49 left; Zul p61.

Grateful acknowledgement is also made to the Theosophical Publishing House of Wheaton, Illinois, USA, for permission to use extracts from *A Still Forest Pool: The Insight Meditation of Achaan Chah*: pp26, 36, 37, 59.

Every reasonable effort has been made to contact copyright owners, but we apologise for any unknown errors or omissions. The list will be corrected, if necessary, in the next reprint.

Illustrations by Tony James Chance pp 28, 29, 35; Robert Goldsmith pp 32, 33, 53; Gillian Hunt pp 15, 25, 30; Tony Morris pp 14, 20, 26, 27; maps by Hardlines.

OXFORD
UNIVERSITY PRESS

Great Clarendon Street, Oxford OX2 6DP
Oxford University Press is a department of the University of Oxford. It furthers the University's objective of excellence in research, scholarship, and education by publishing worldwide in

Oxford New York

Auckland Bangkok Buenos Aires Cape Town Chennai Dar es Salaam Delhi Hong Kong Istanbul Karachi Kolkata Kuala Lumpur Madrid Melbourne Mexico City Mumbai Nairobi São Paulo Shanghai Taipei Tokyo Toronto

Oxford is a registered trade mark of Oxford University Press in the UK and in certain other countries

British Library Cataloguing in Publication Data available

ISBN 0 19 917241 2

Printed in Singapore by KHL Printing Co Pte Ltd